COLORS

of

THE SKY

Images from Texas

By Nick Stockland

A special thanks to Marcy McGuire for providing valuable artistic direction in the formatting of this book. This is my eighth opportunity to work with Marcy, on both children's books and photography books – two very different styles indeed. Once again her contribution is essential, and excellent.

Also a special thanks to Romana Bovan for an exceptional design on the book cover, and Sunny Ramirez for providing the image from deep in the Texas hill country. This is my first opportunity to work with Romana, and I sincerely appreciate his contribution and artistic vision.

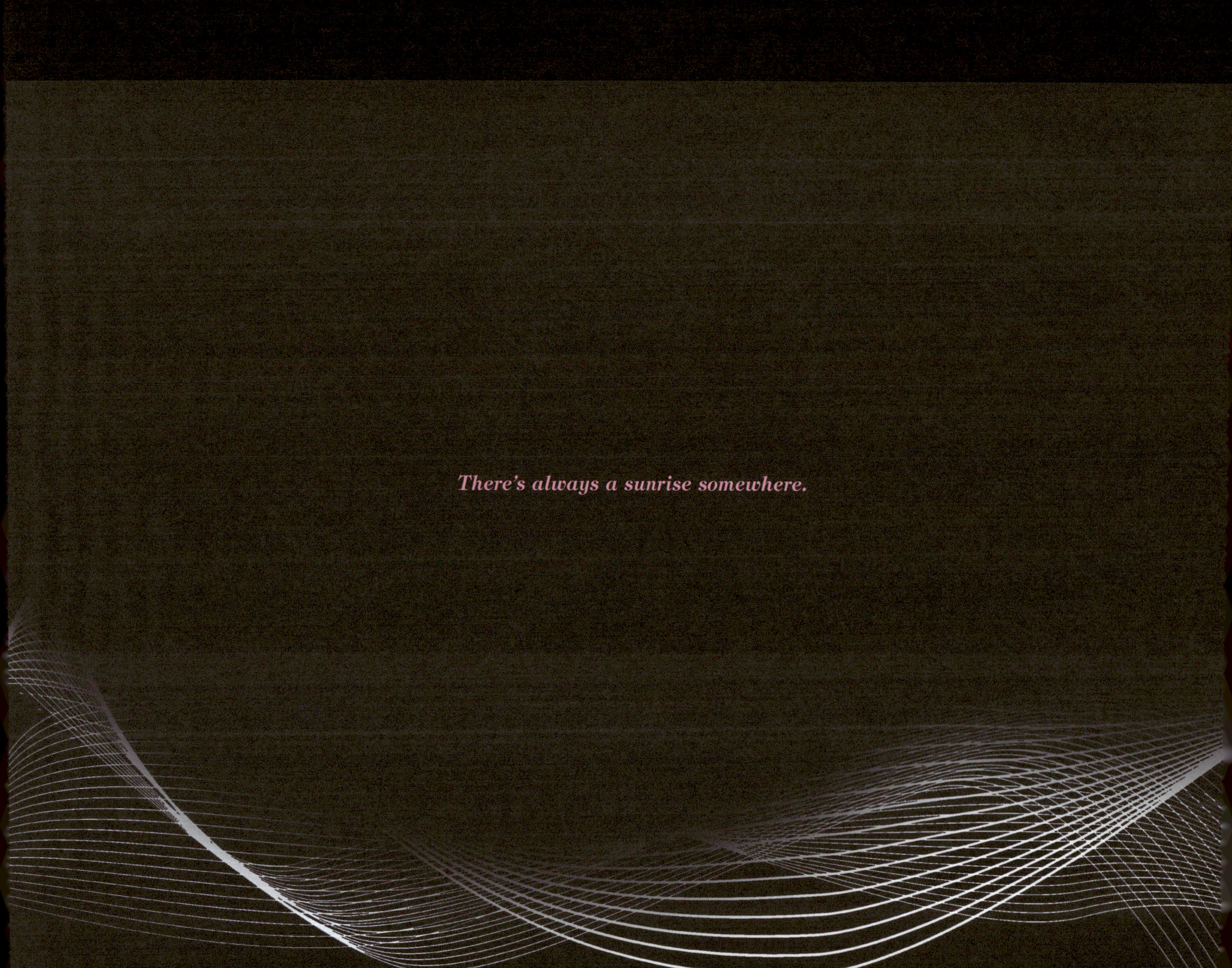
There's always a sunrise somewhere.

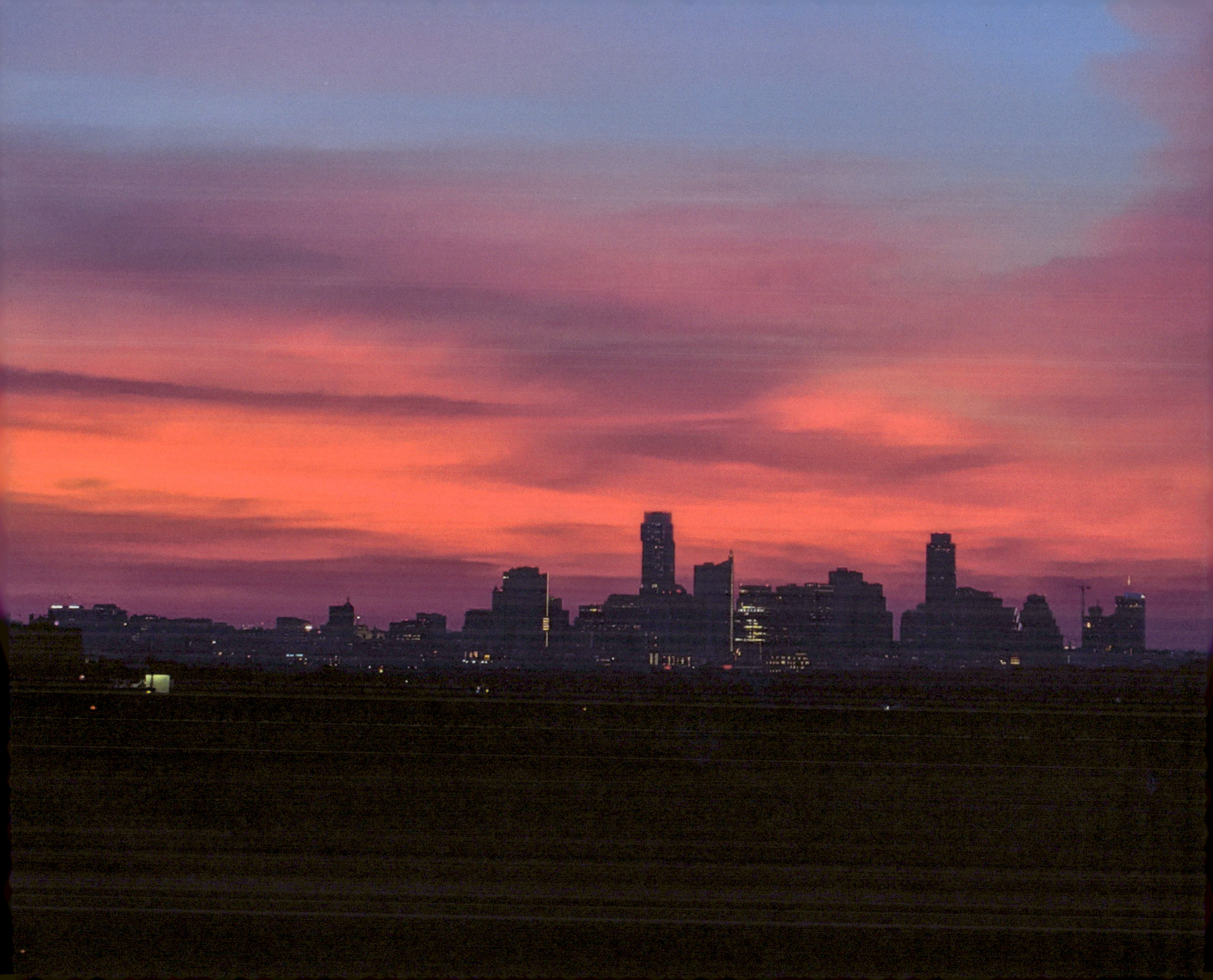

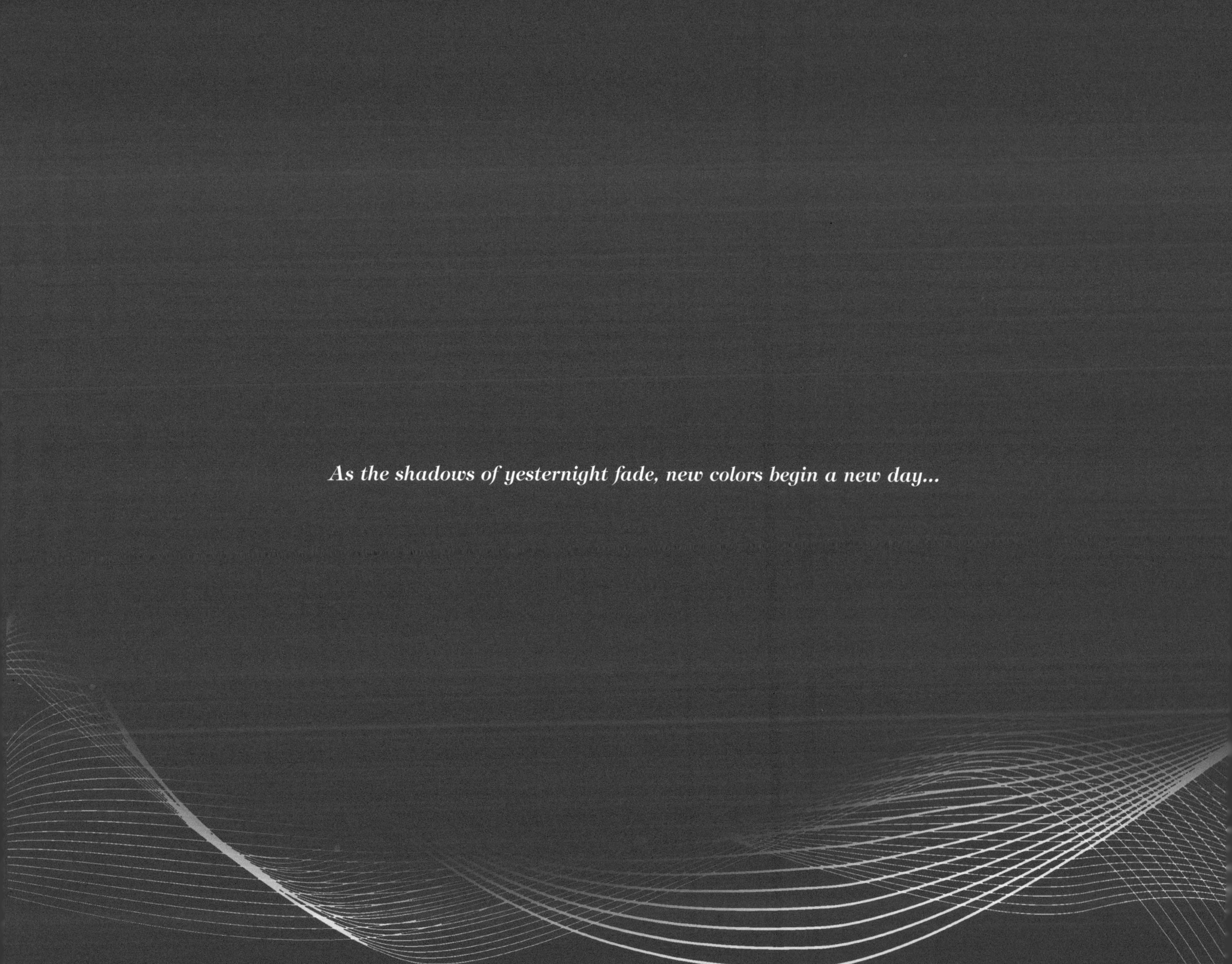

As the shadows of yesternight fade, new colors begin a new day...

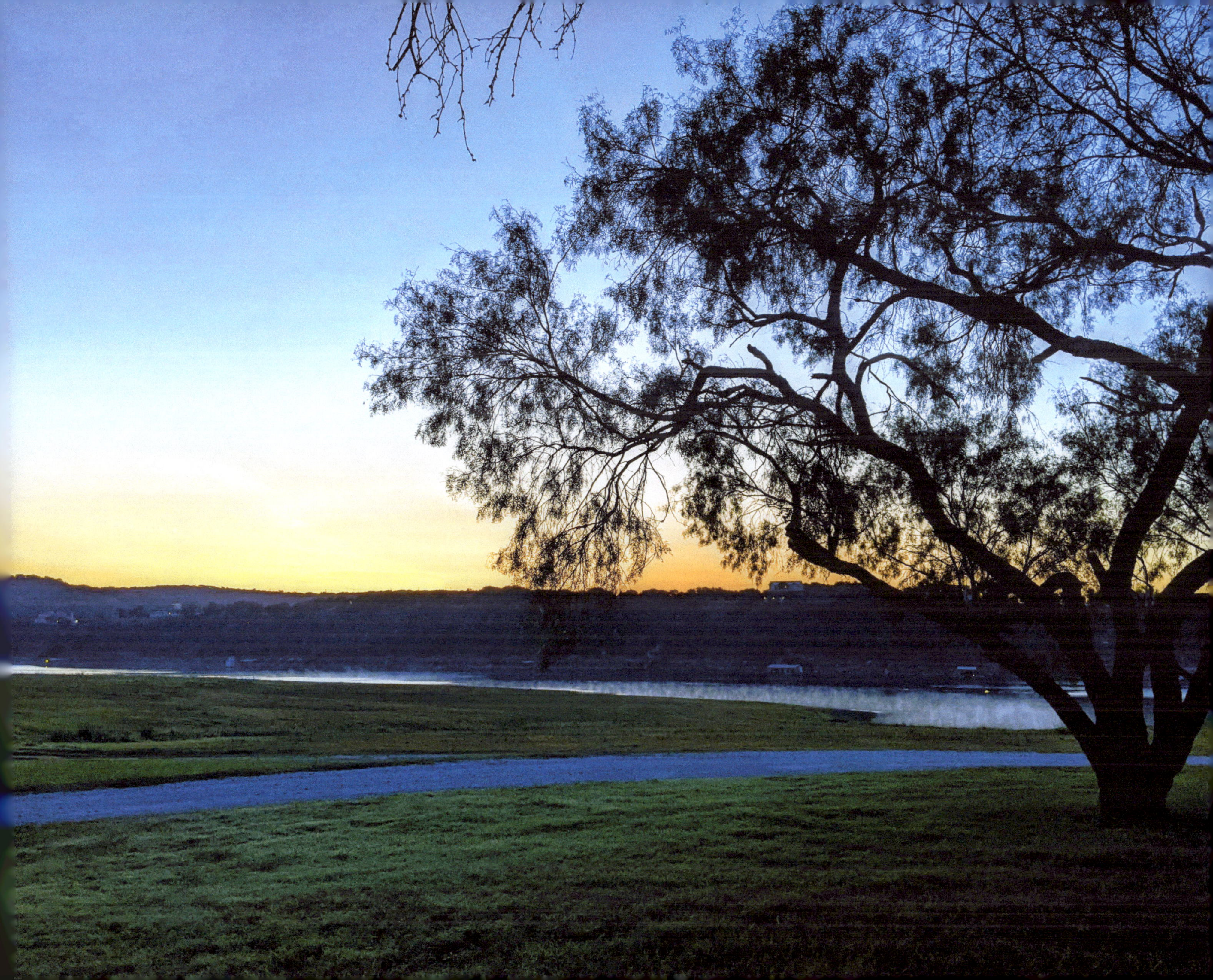

*The sun rises for the city, and it rises for the trees, as the city
awakens, along with the nature around it.*

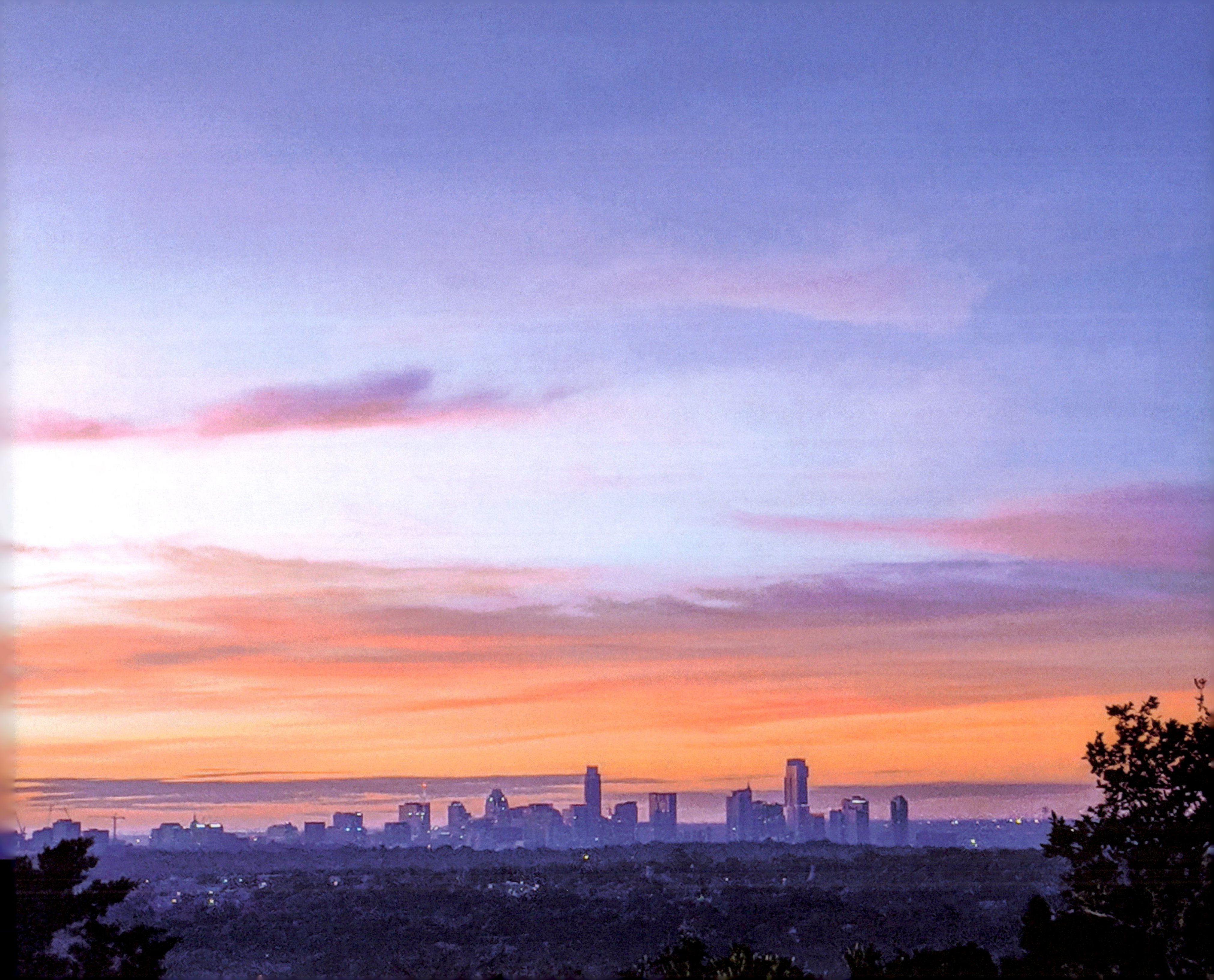

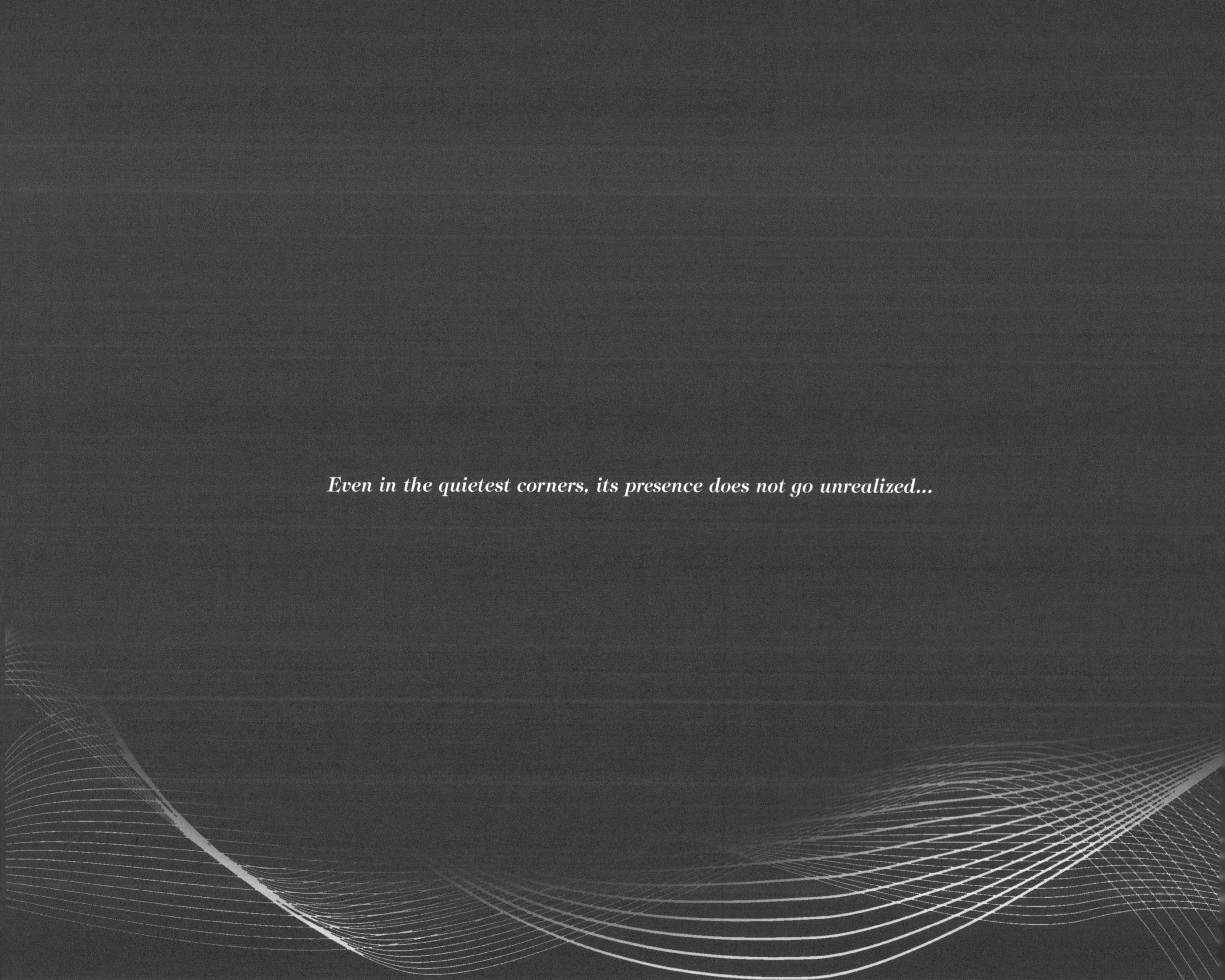

Even in the quietest corners, its presence does not go unrealized...

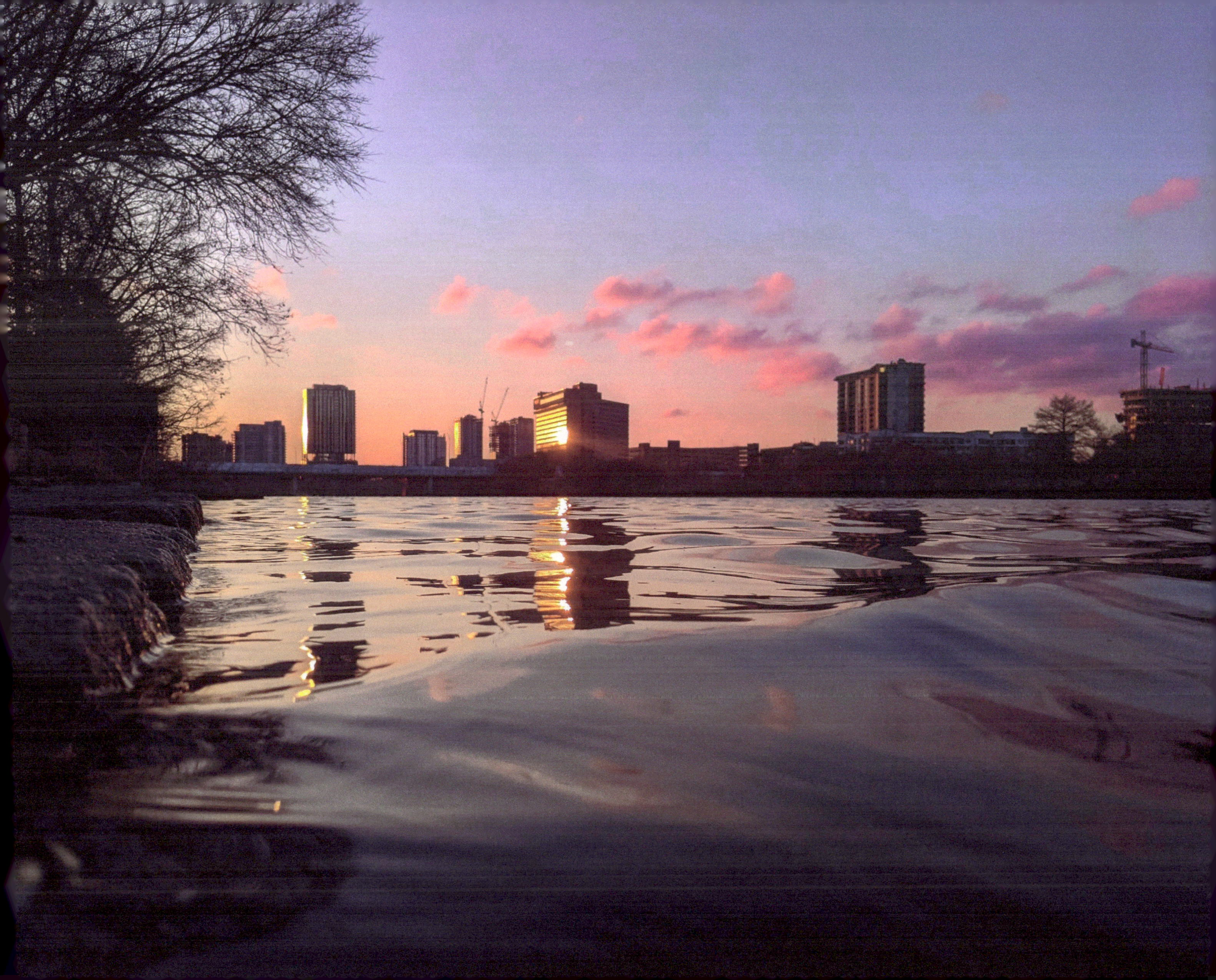

As the vast of night gives way to a new brilliance.

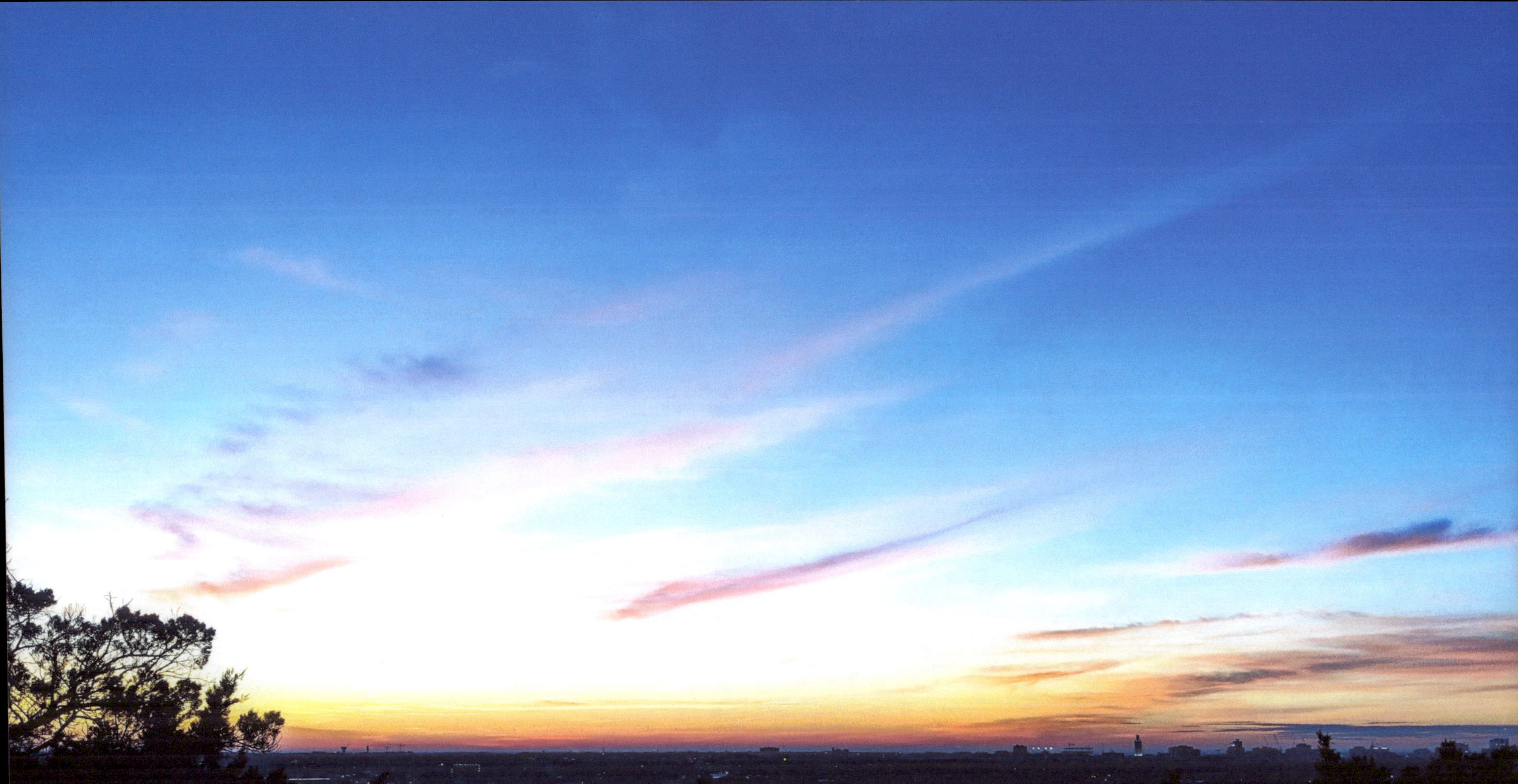

Sea and land, near and far away, no territory is unaffected.

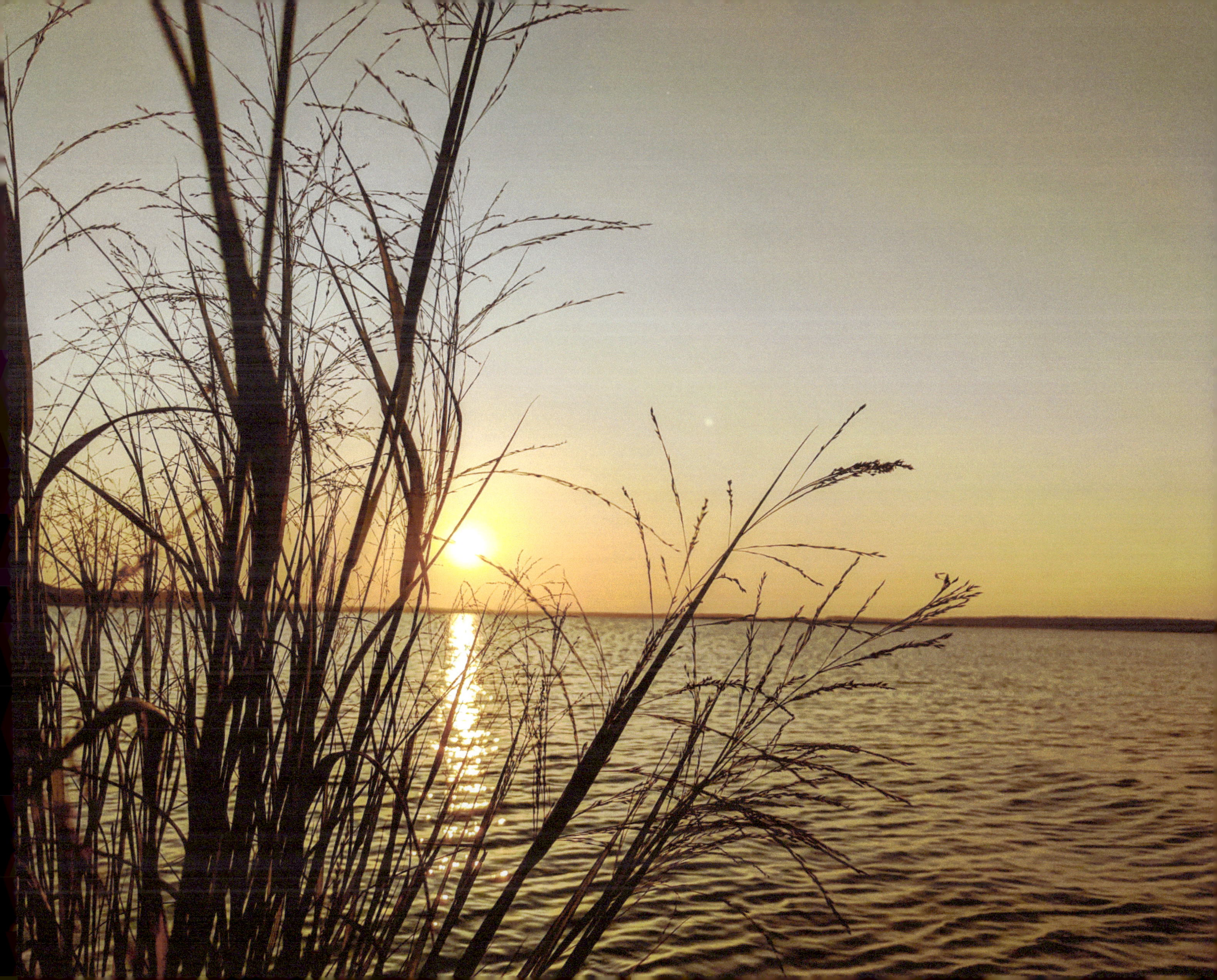

These pieces of creation – every grain of sand, every speck of mist, every shell – takes notice.

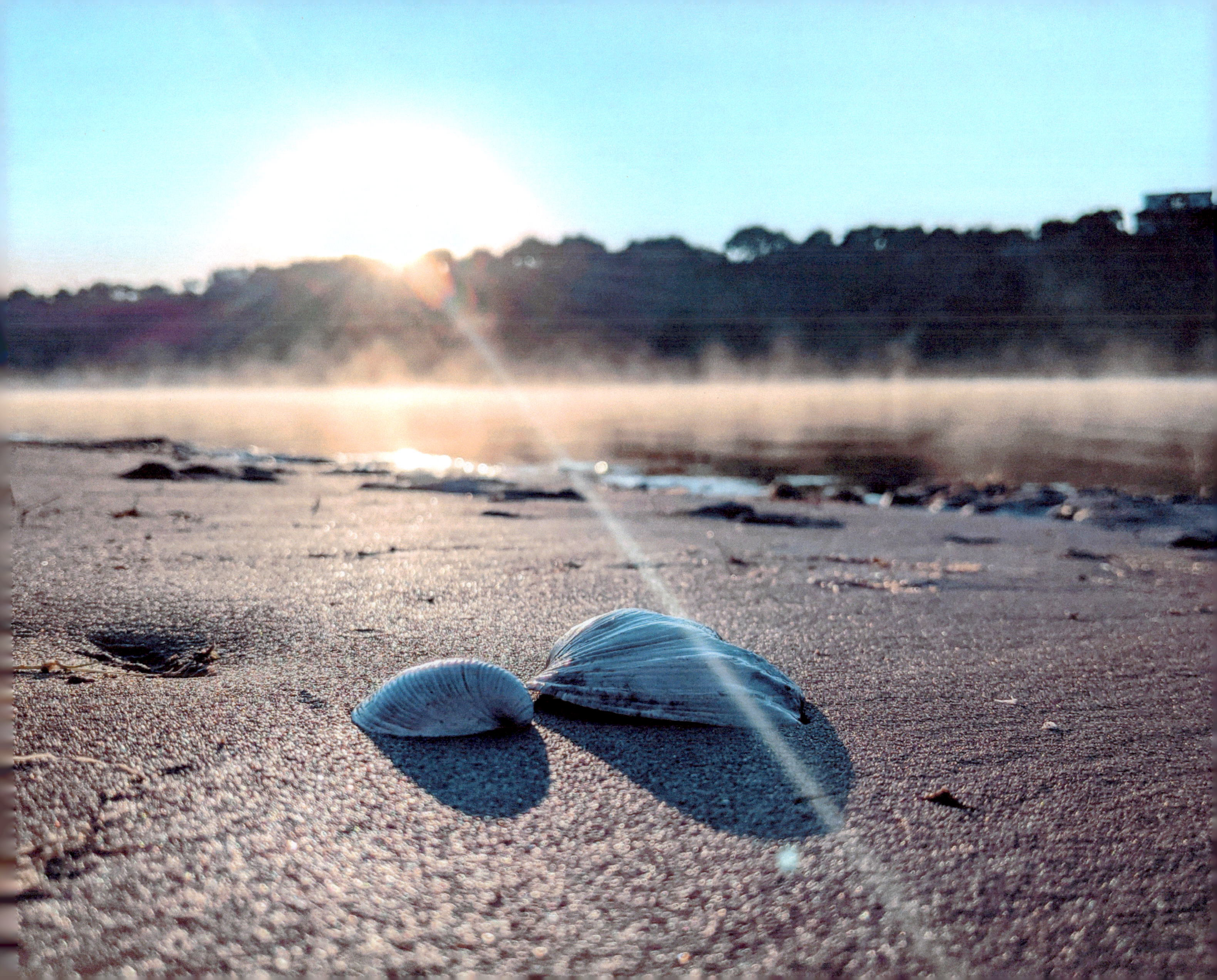

The sun rises for the water, and it rises for the earth.

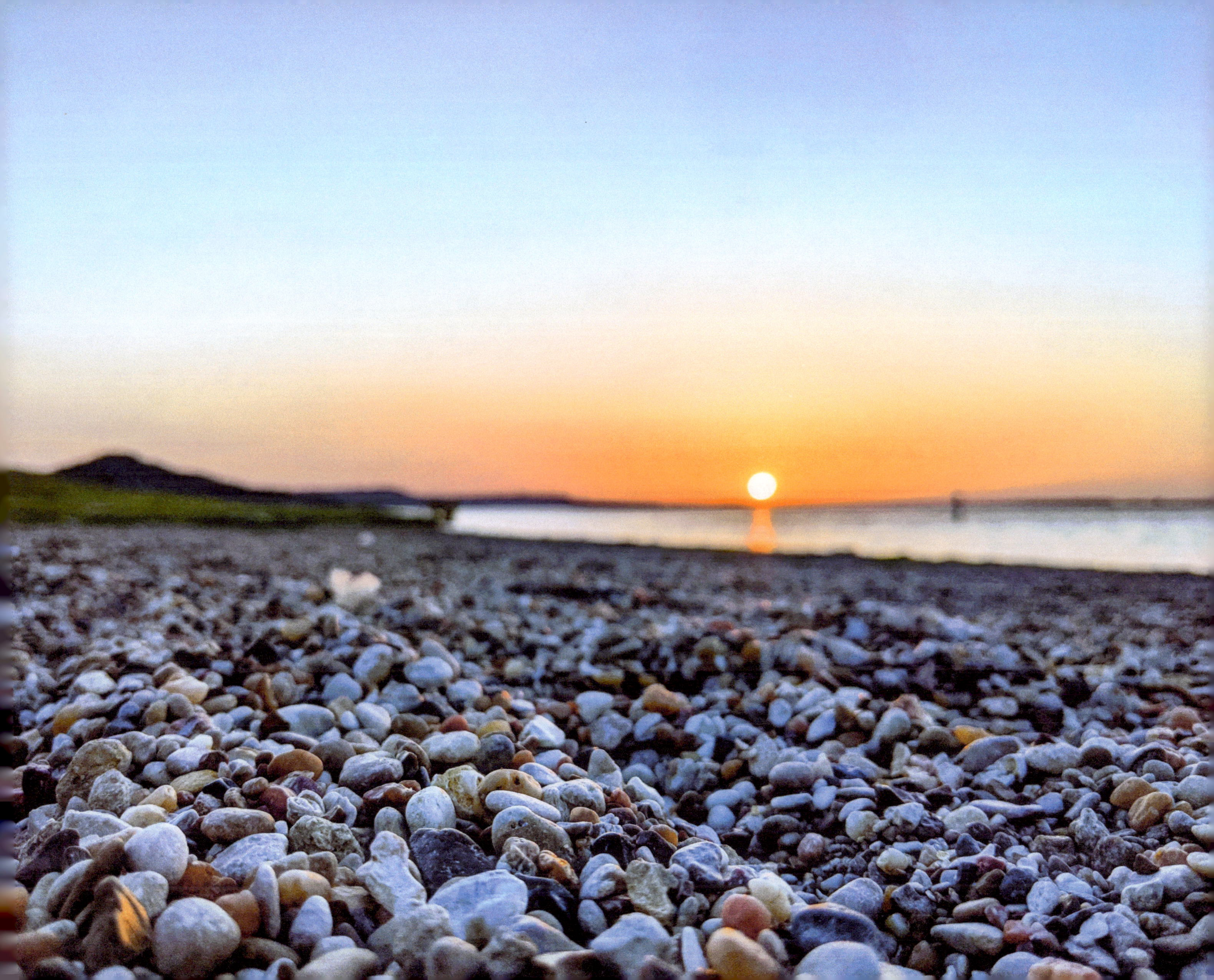

By which even the smallest plant is given its life...

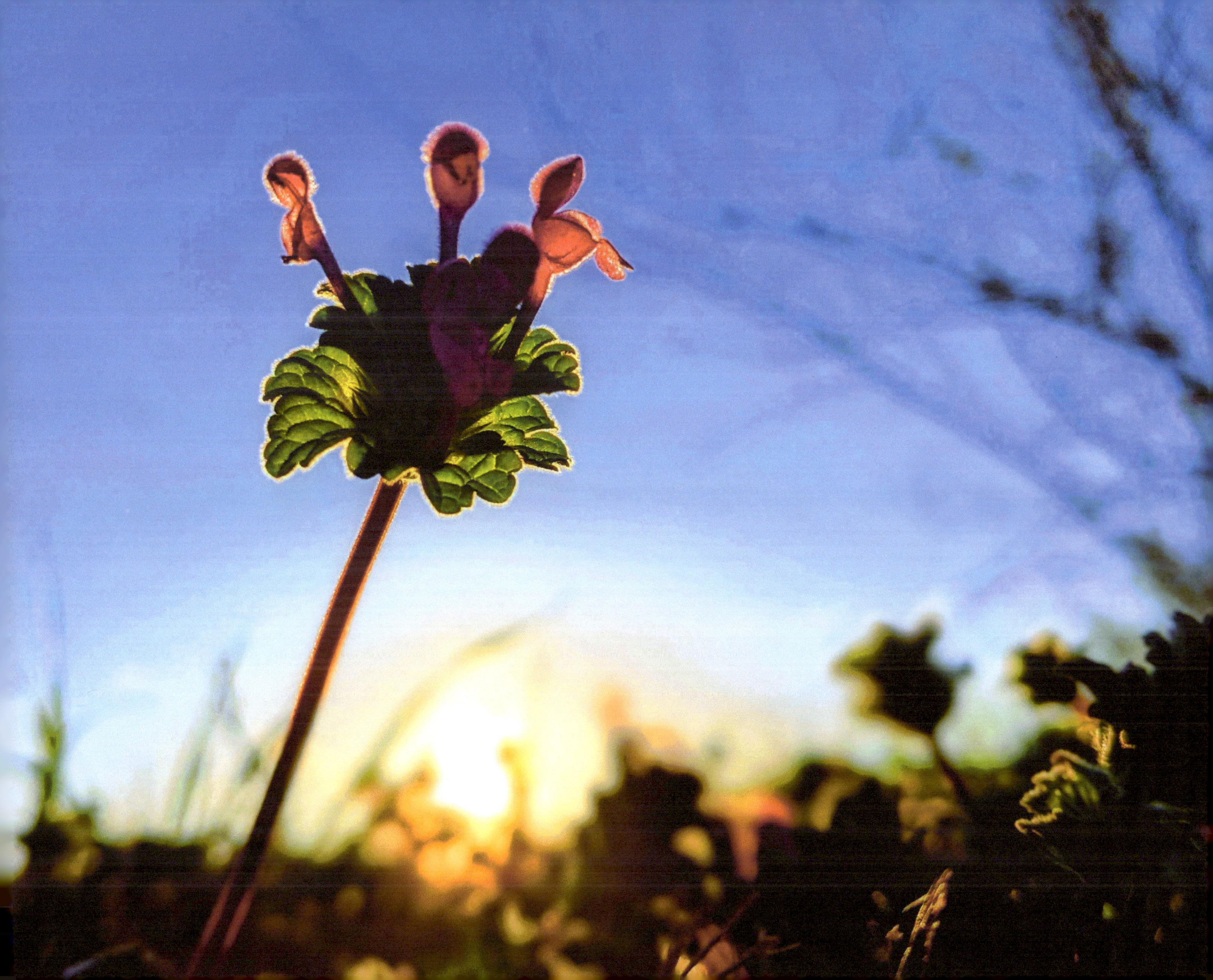

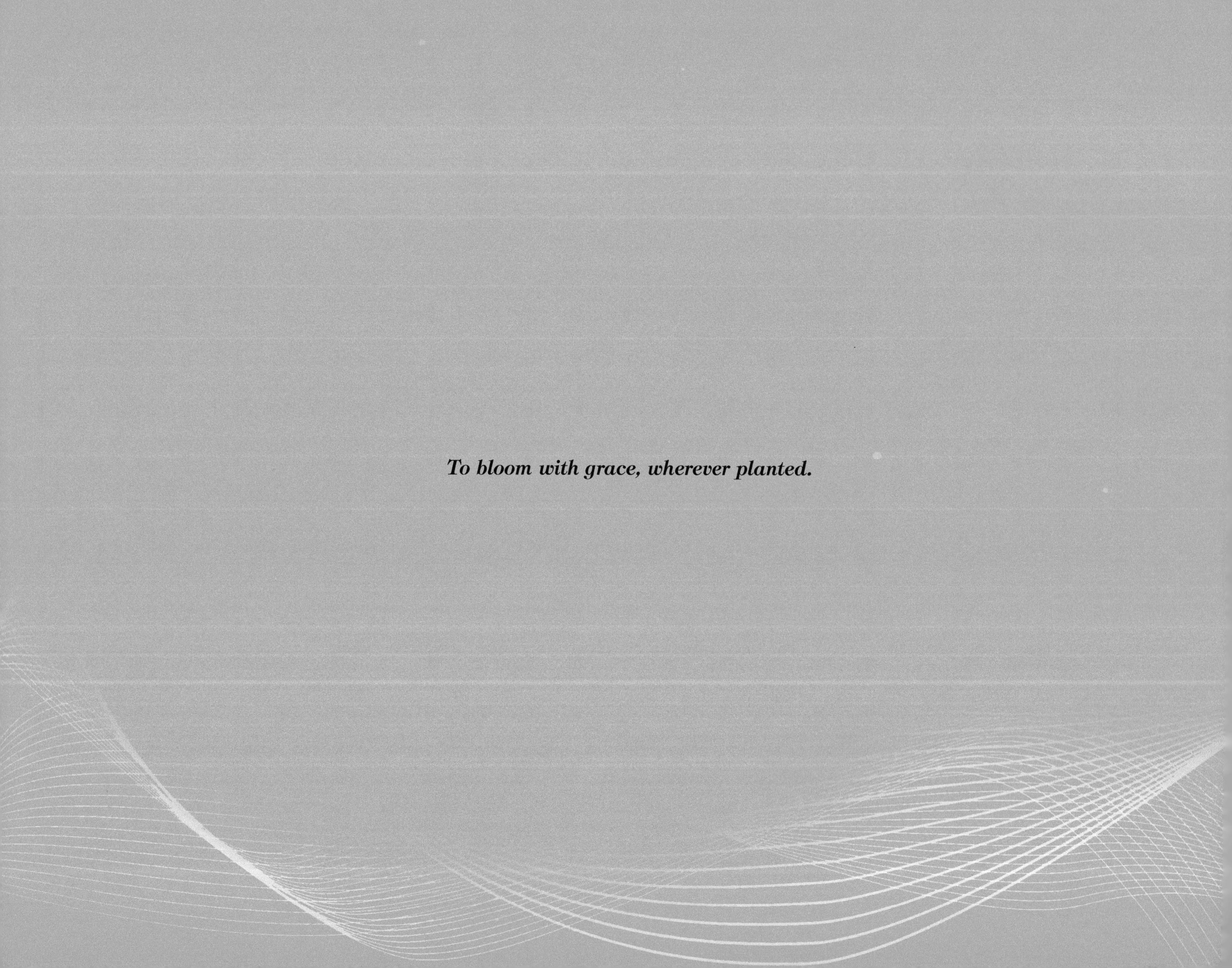

To bloom with grace, wherever planted.

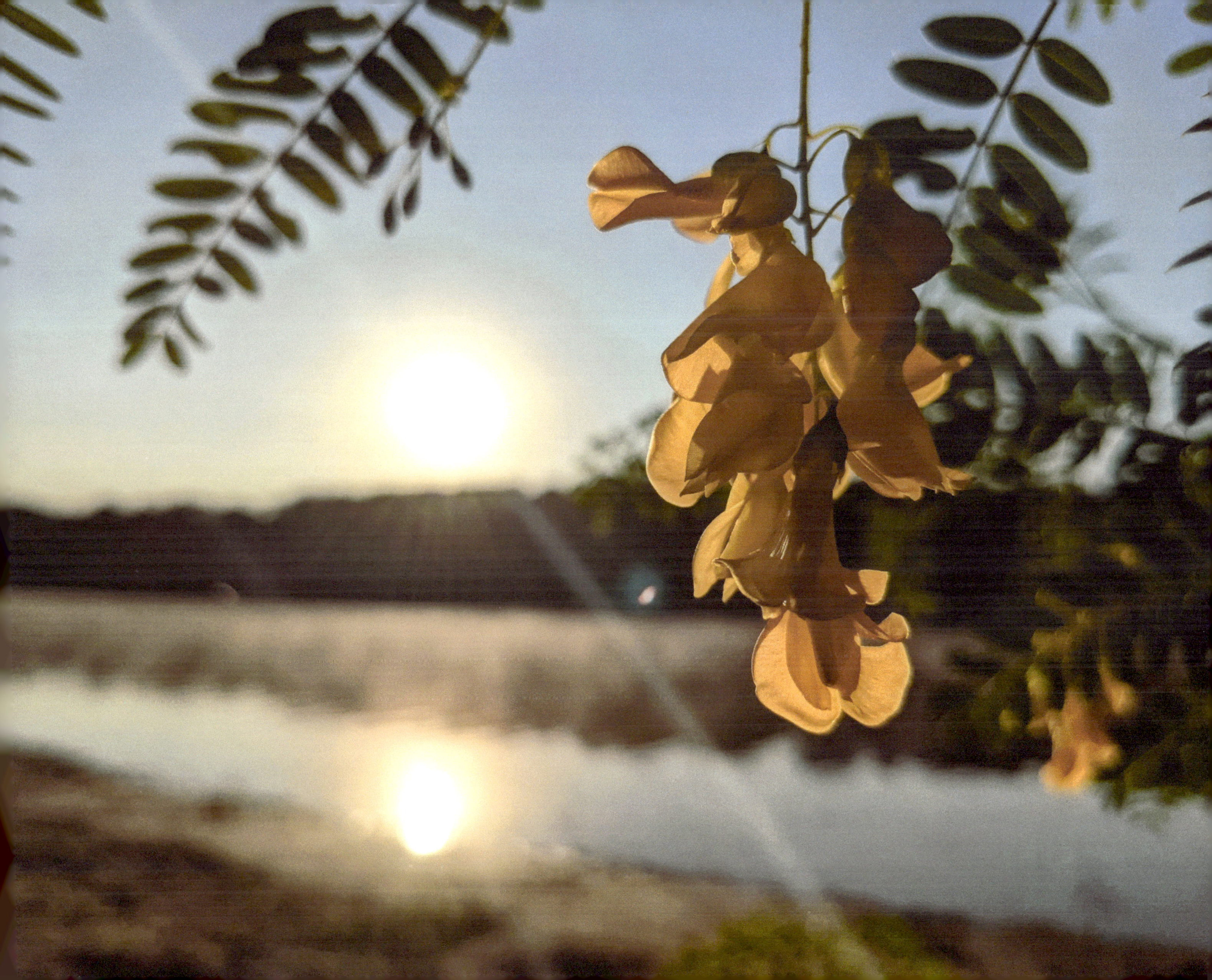

Along with every storied piece of wood, once a majestic tree...

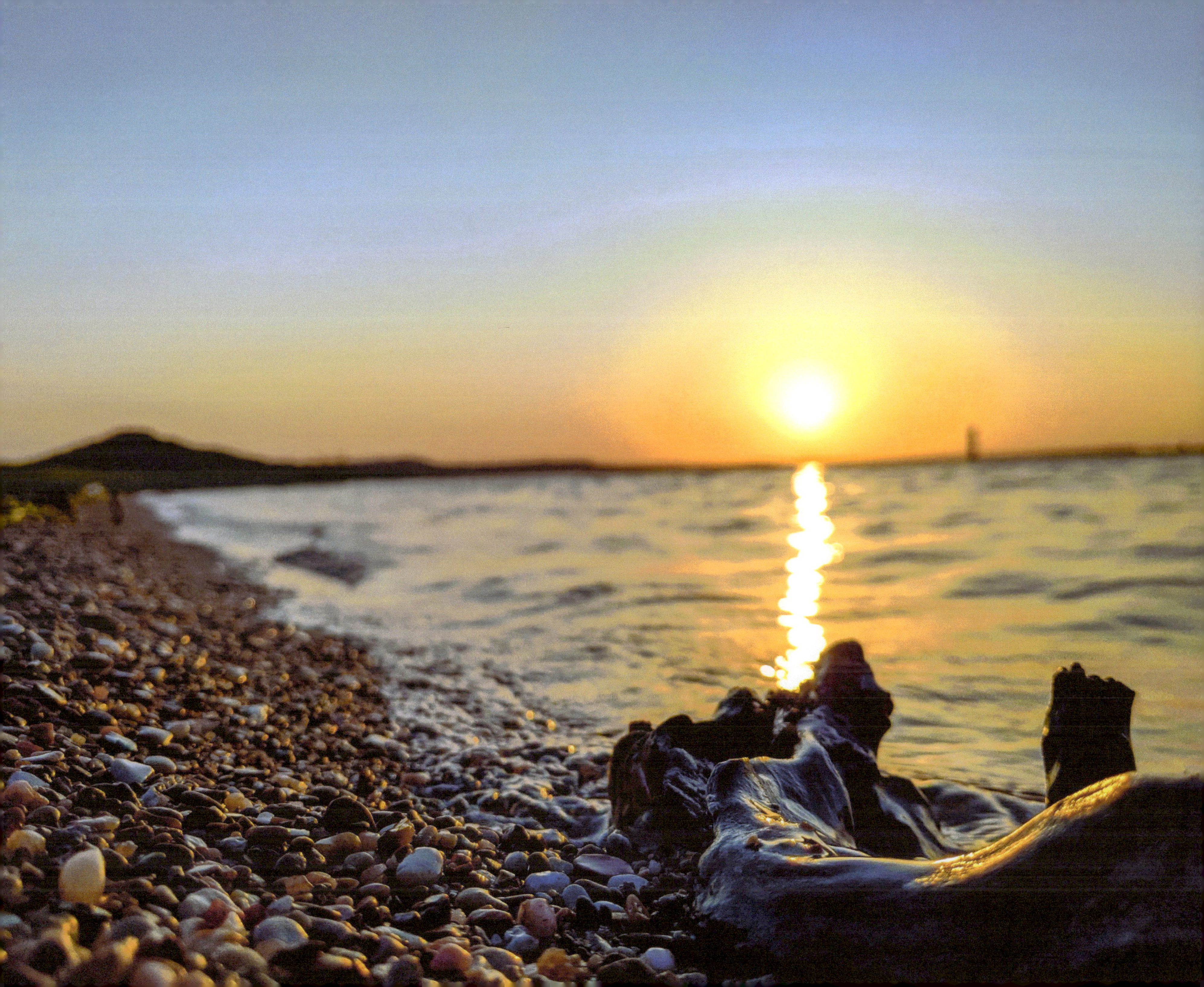

*And every weathered rock, its age unknown,
sculpted by light, heat, and water.*

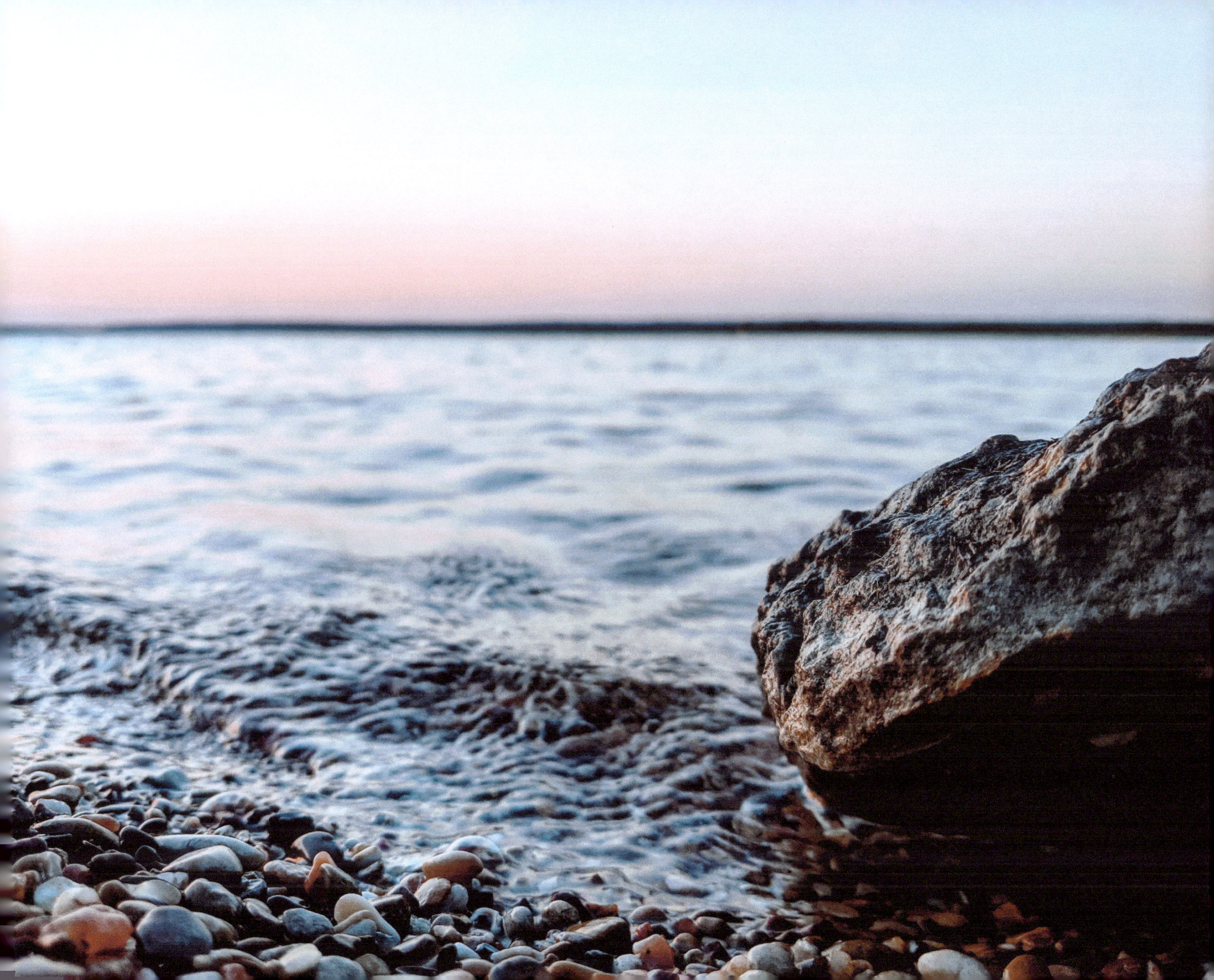

*Potential follows the sunrise, untethered from the
limits of our comprehension*

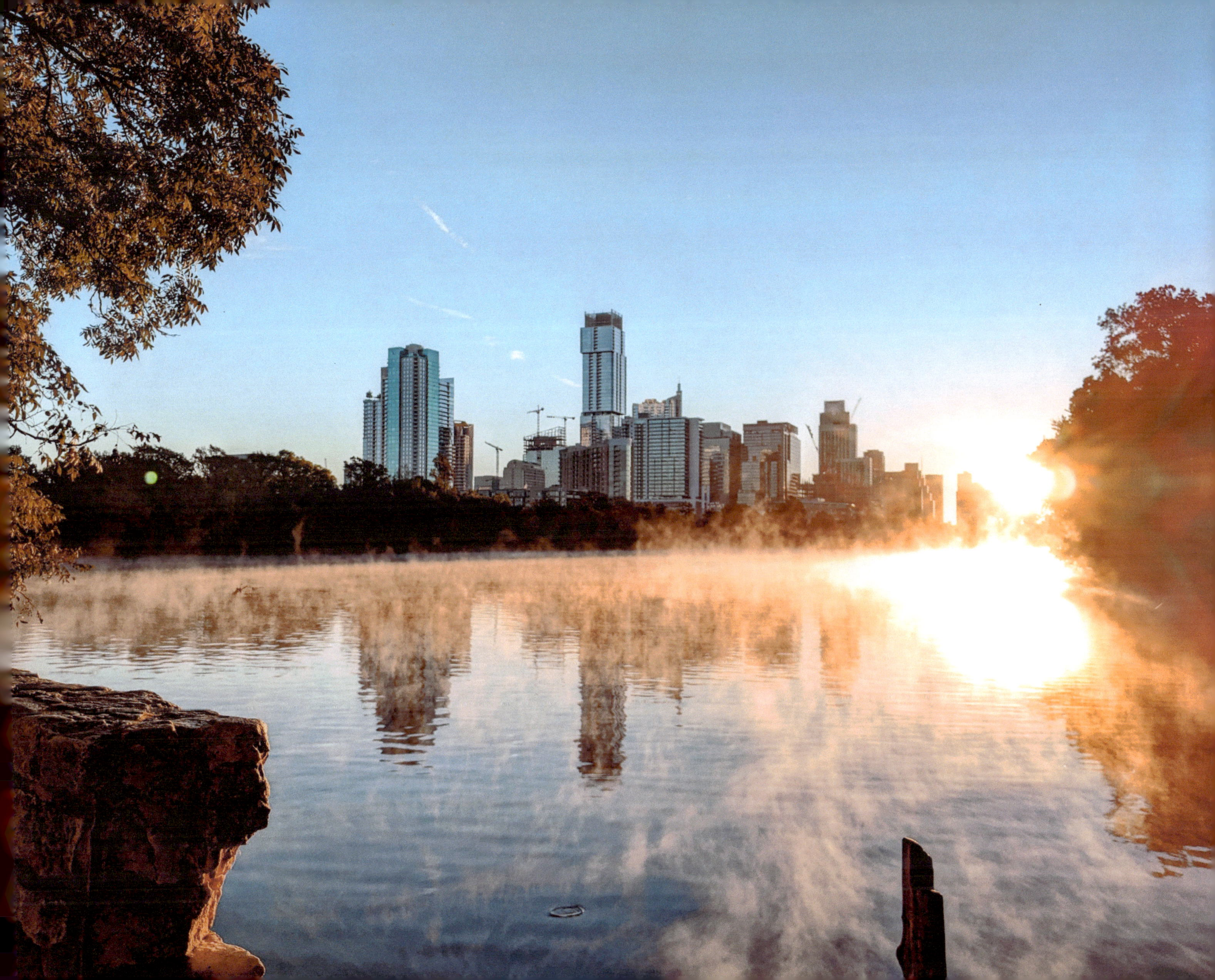

Dawn and dusk are both given their time.

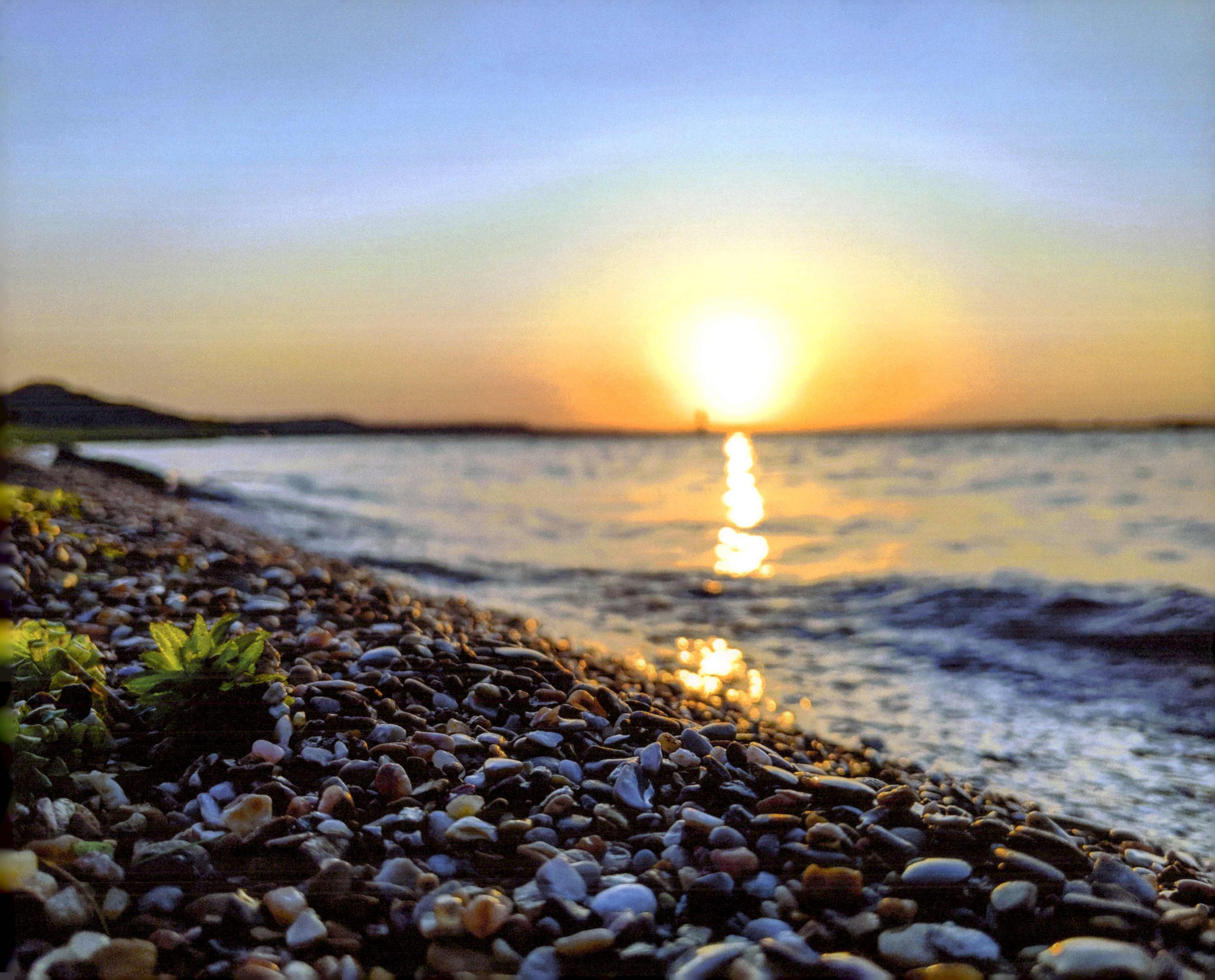

As the sun sets for the earth, gifting the day and all that it gave us.

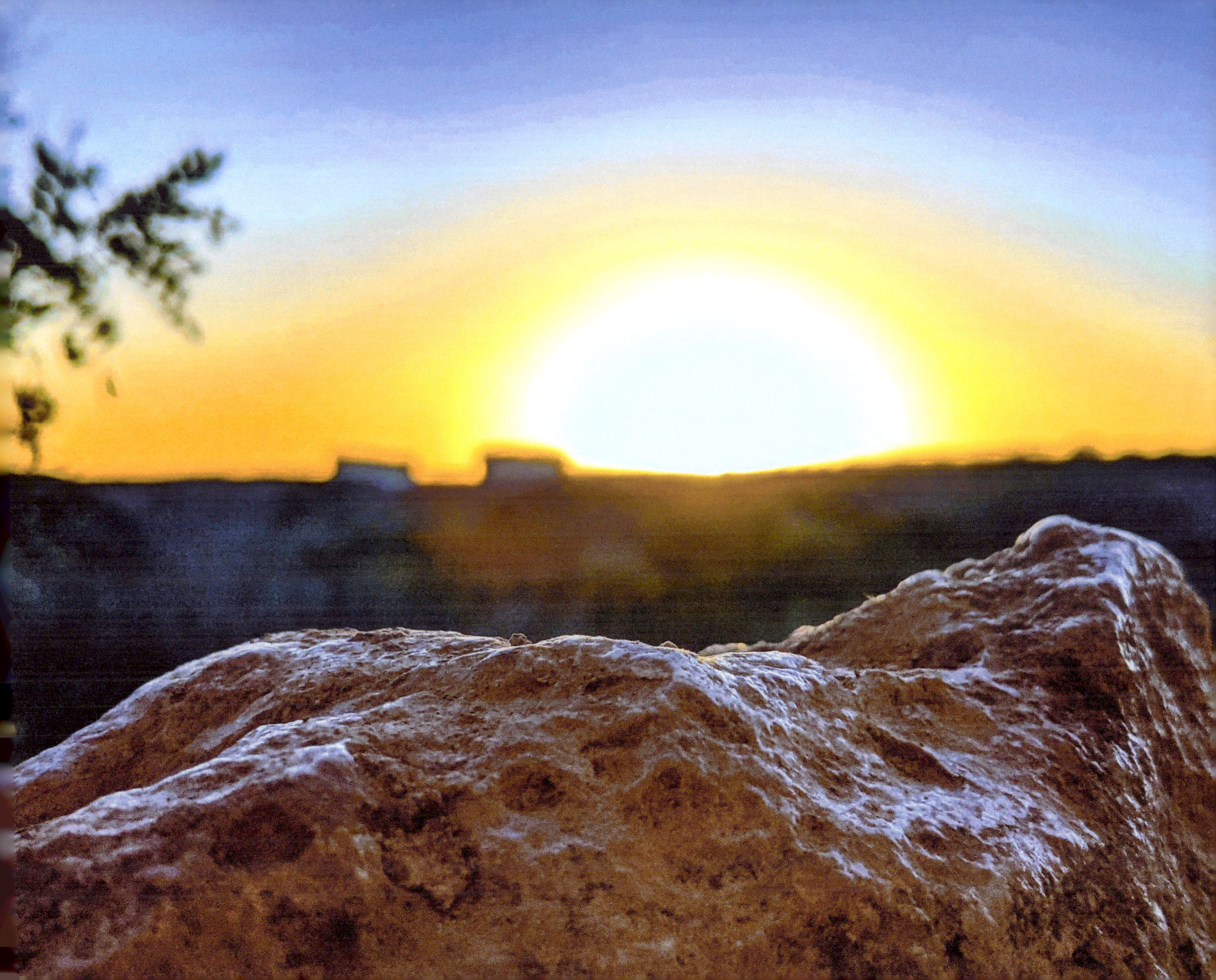

Another essential piece to creation, as the rocks and the trees know.

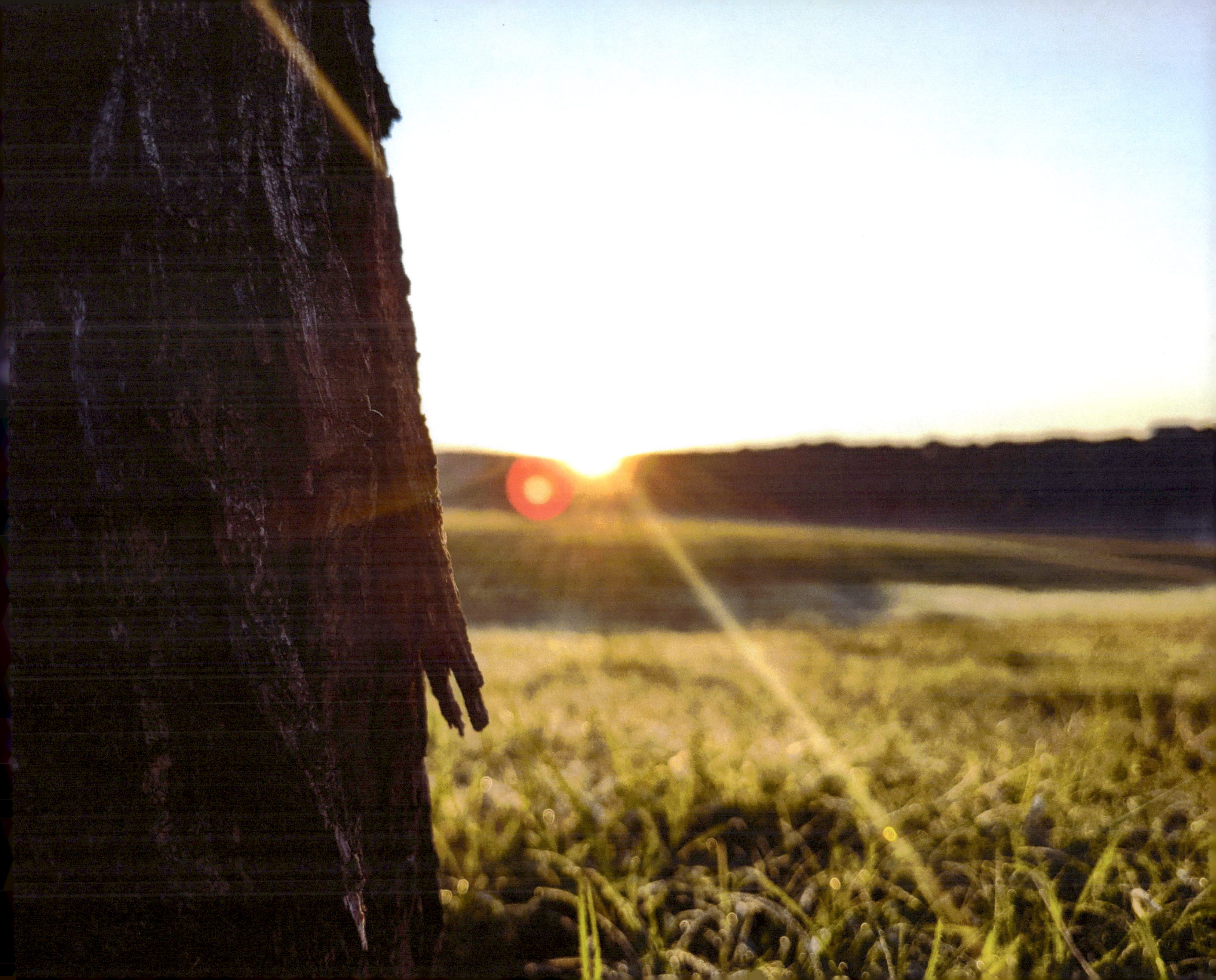

Inspiration balanced by sentiment, spirit balanced by heart.

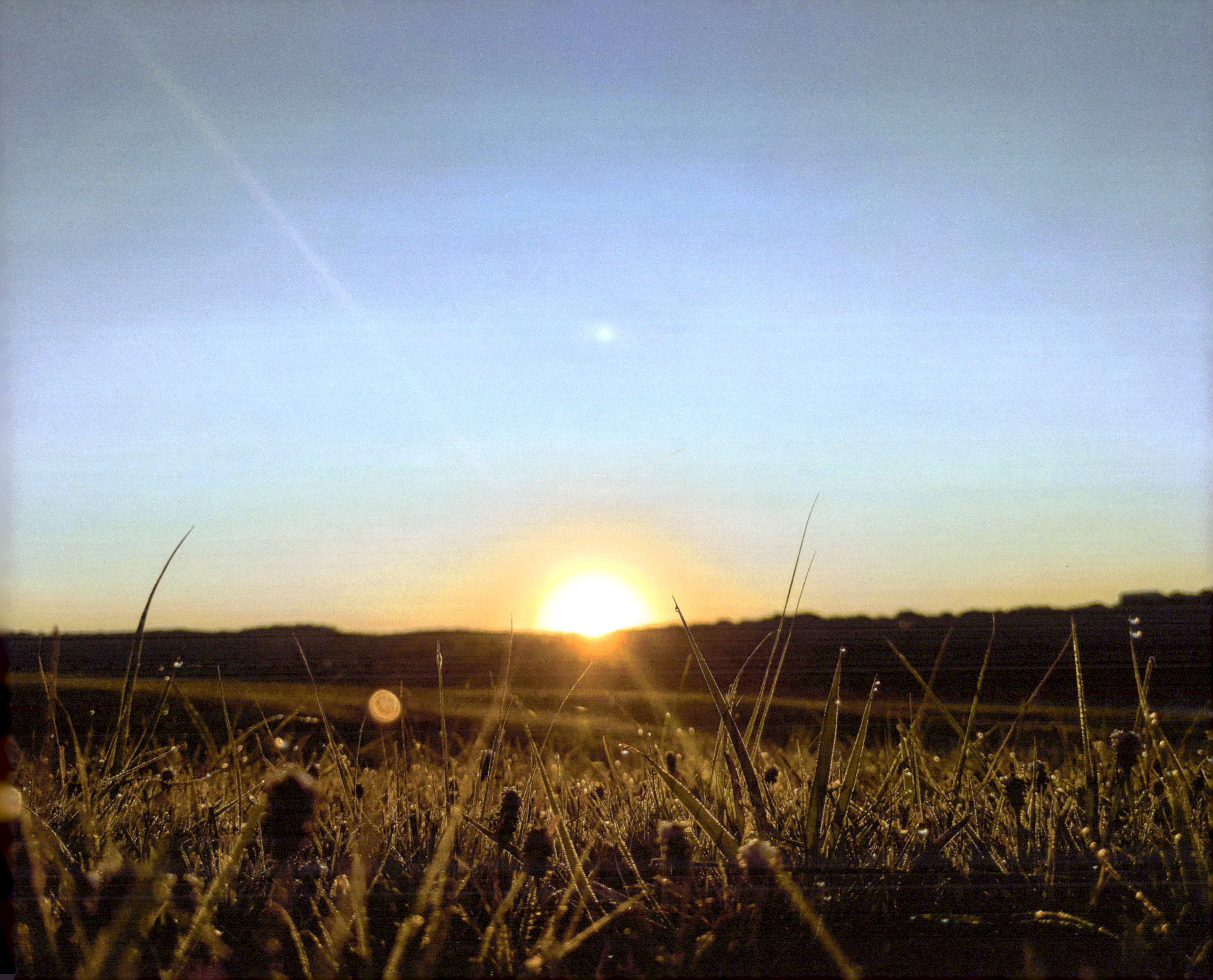

These patterns say many things, unique to the beholder.

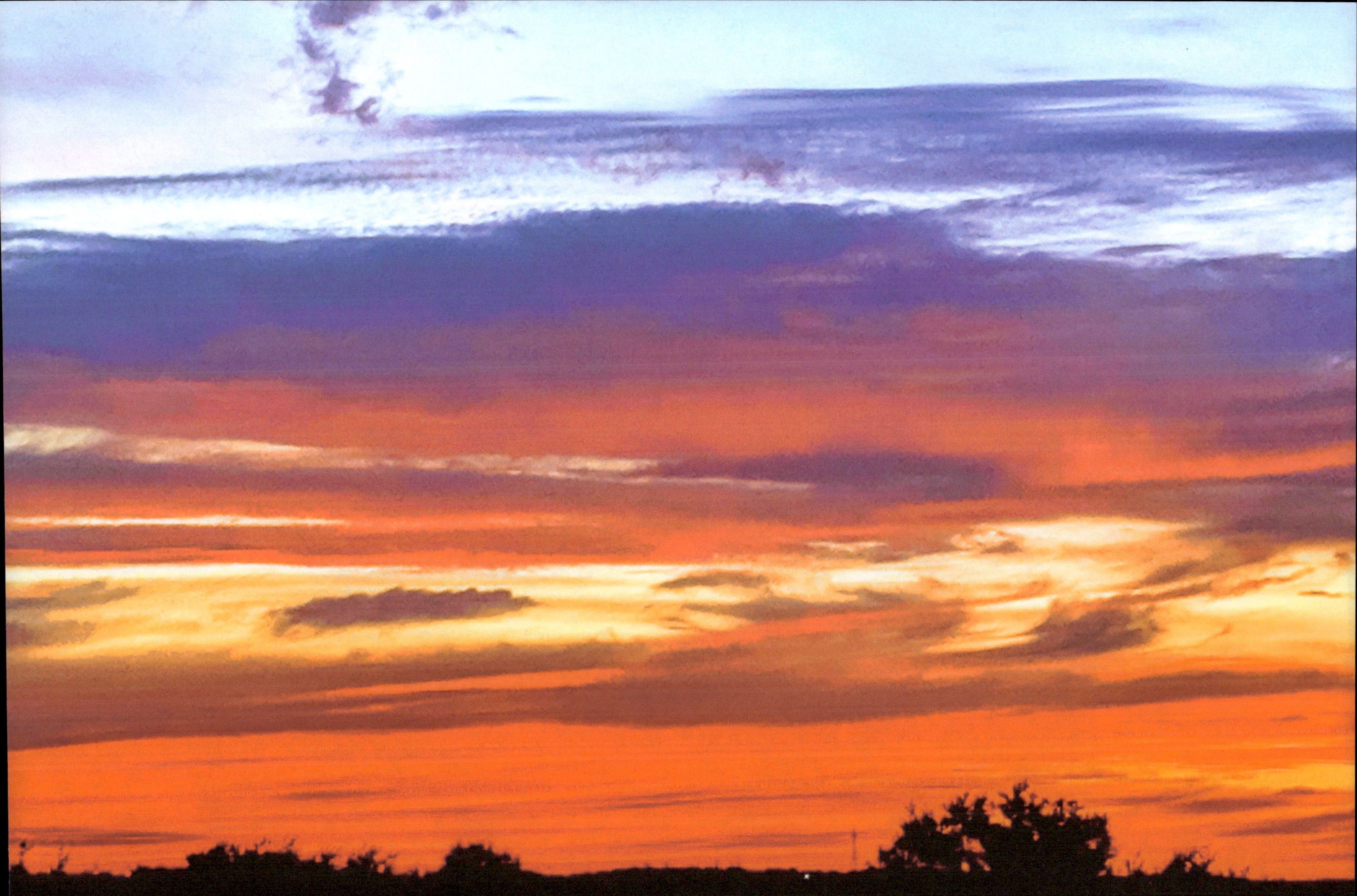

These moments — existing briefly, then never to be replicated again.

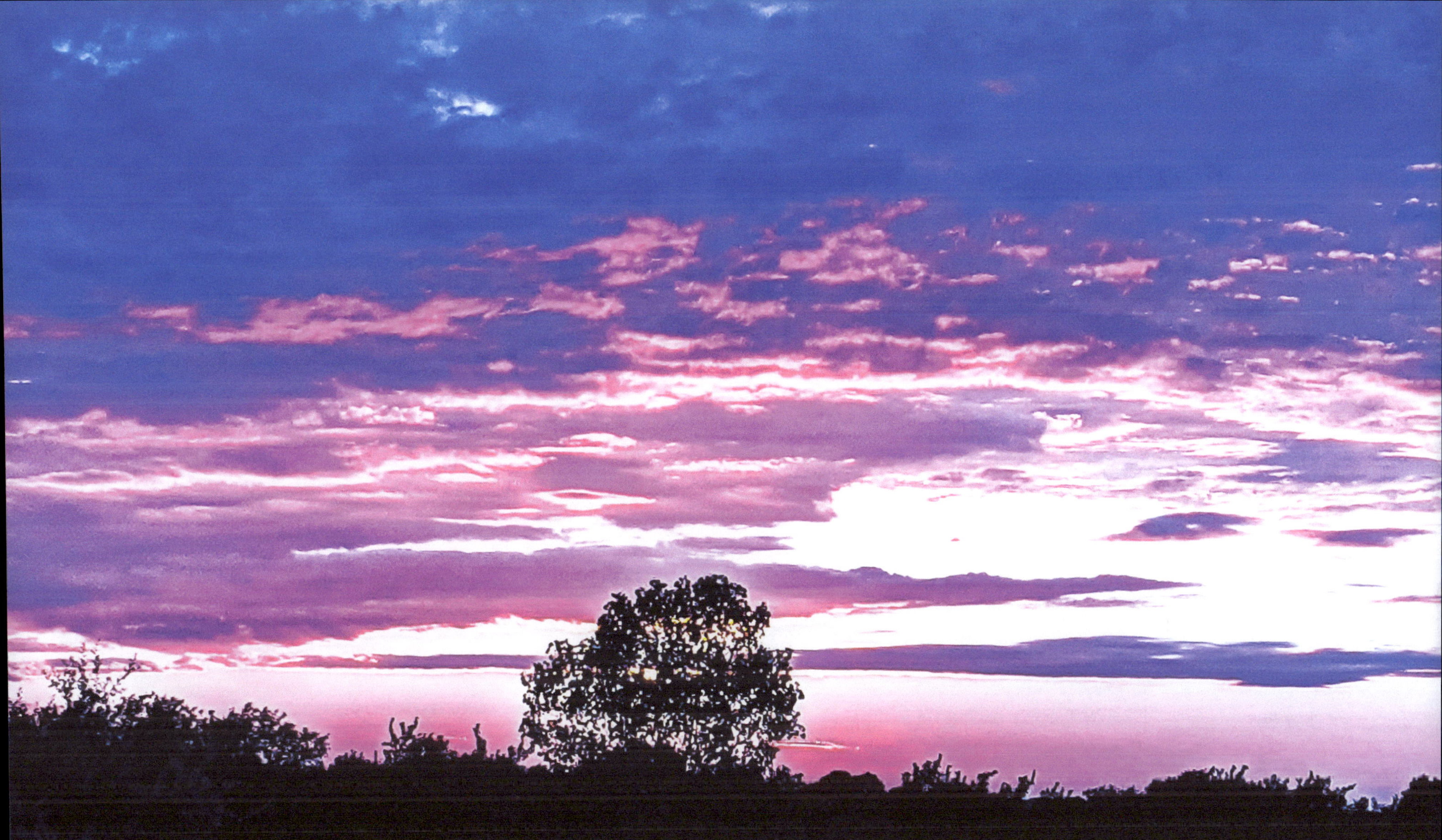

This too is creation, these colors of the sky.

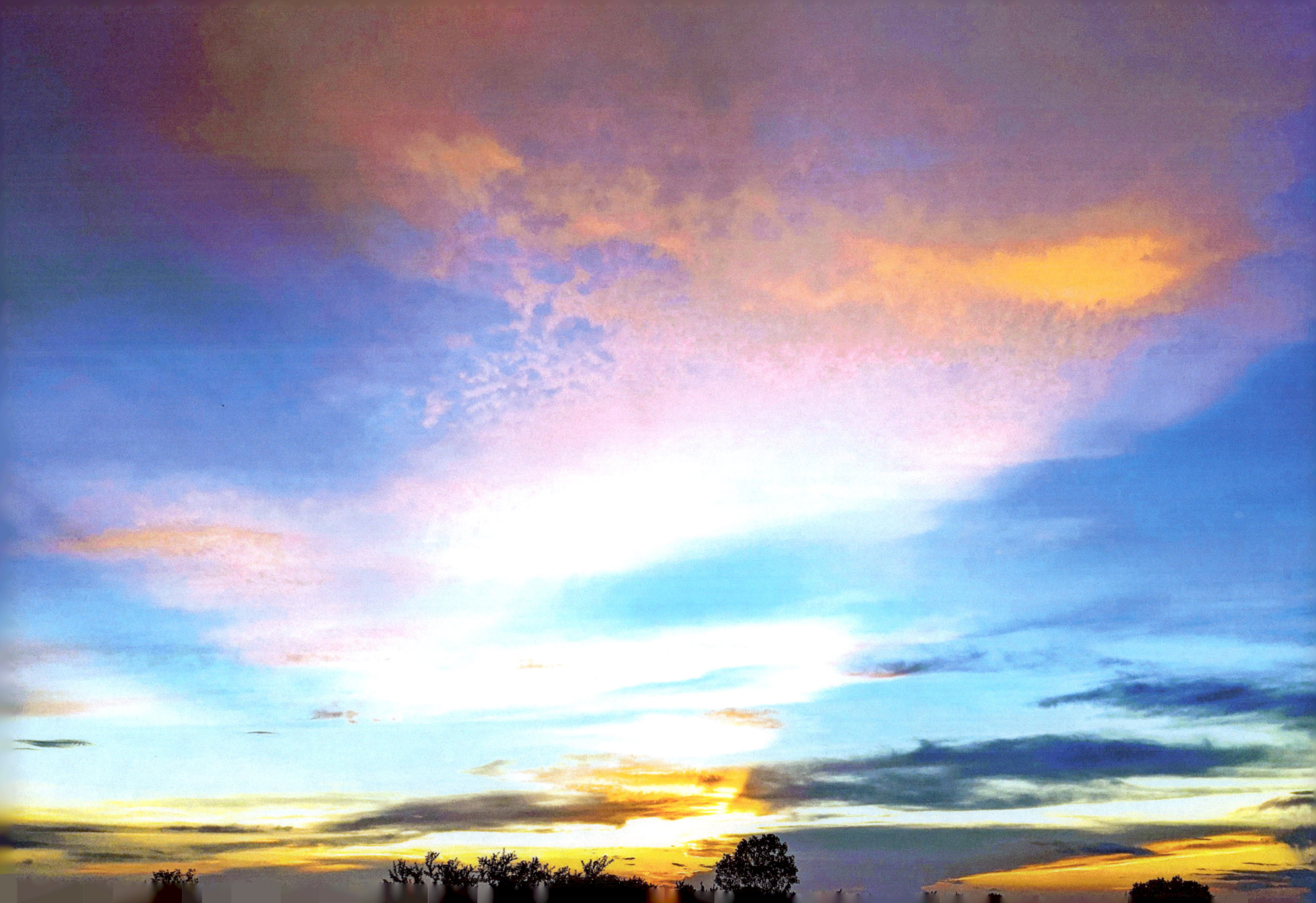

And soon the stars will make themselves known,
as the sun departs with one last glimpse, to finish the day.

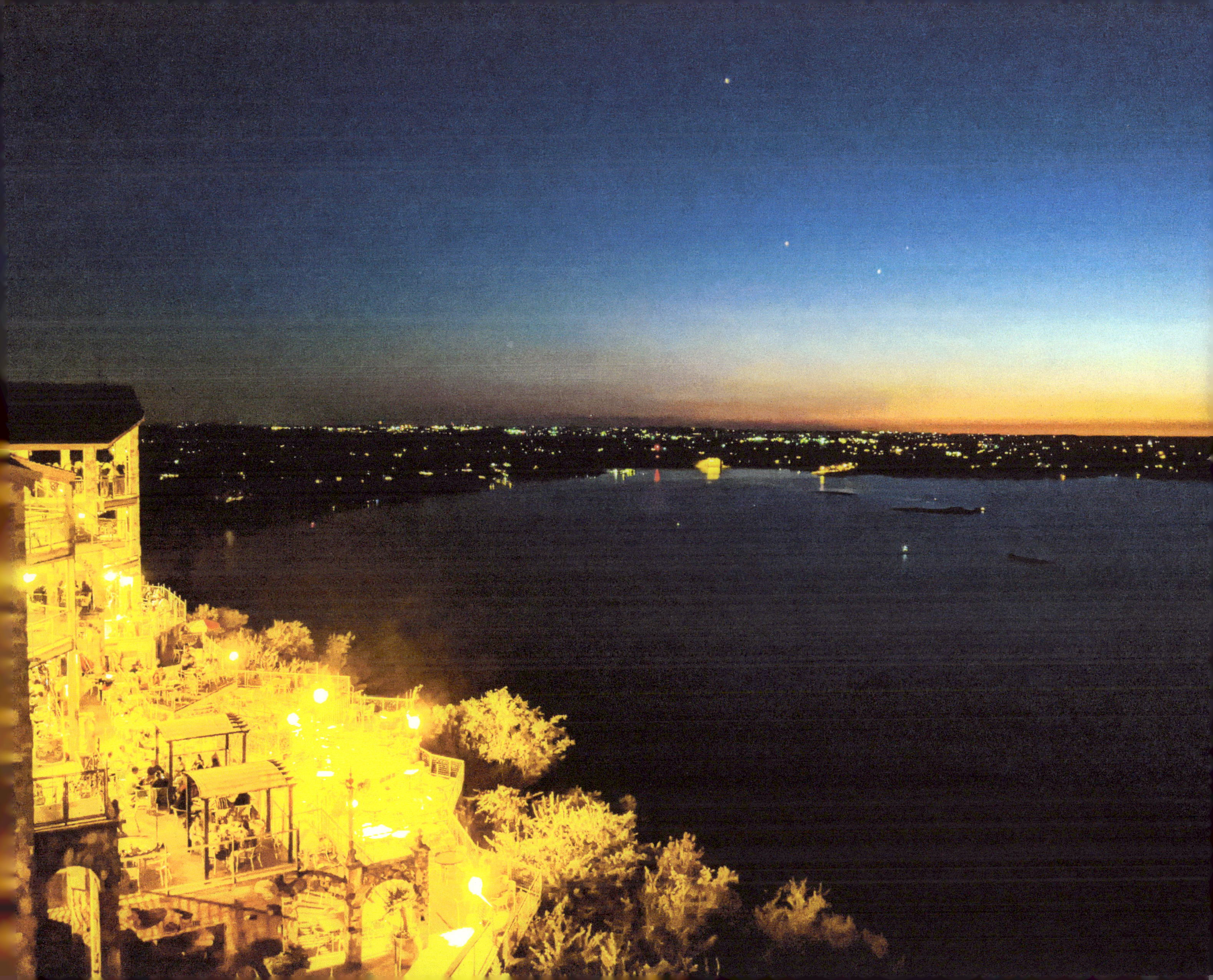

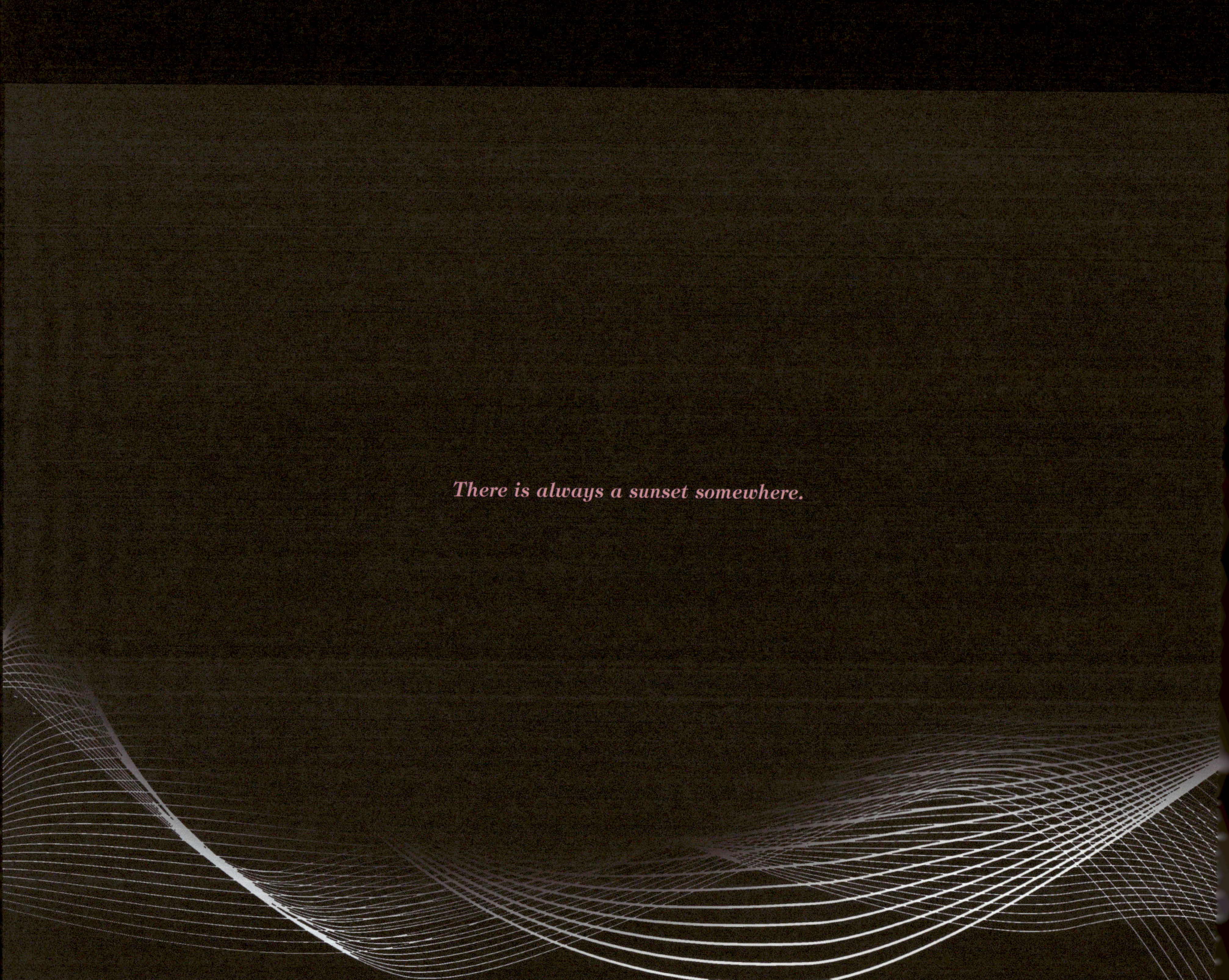

There is always a sunset somewhere.

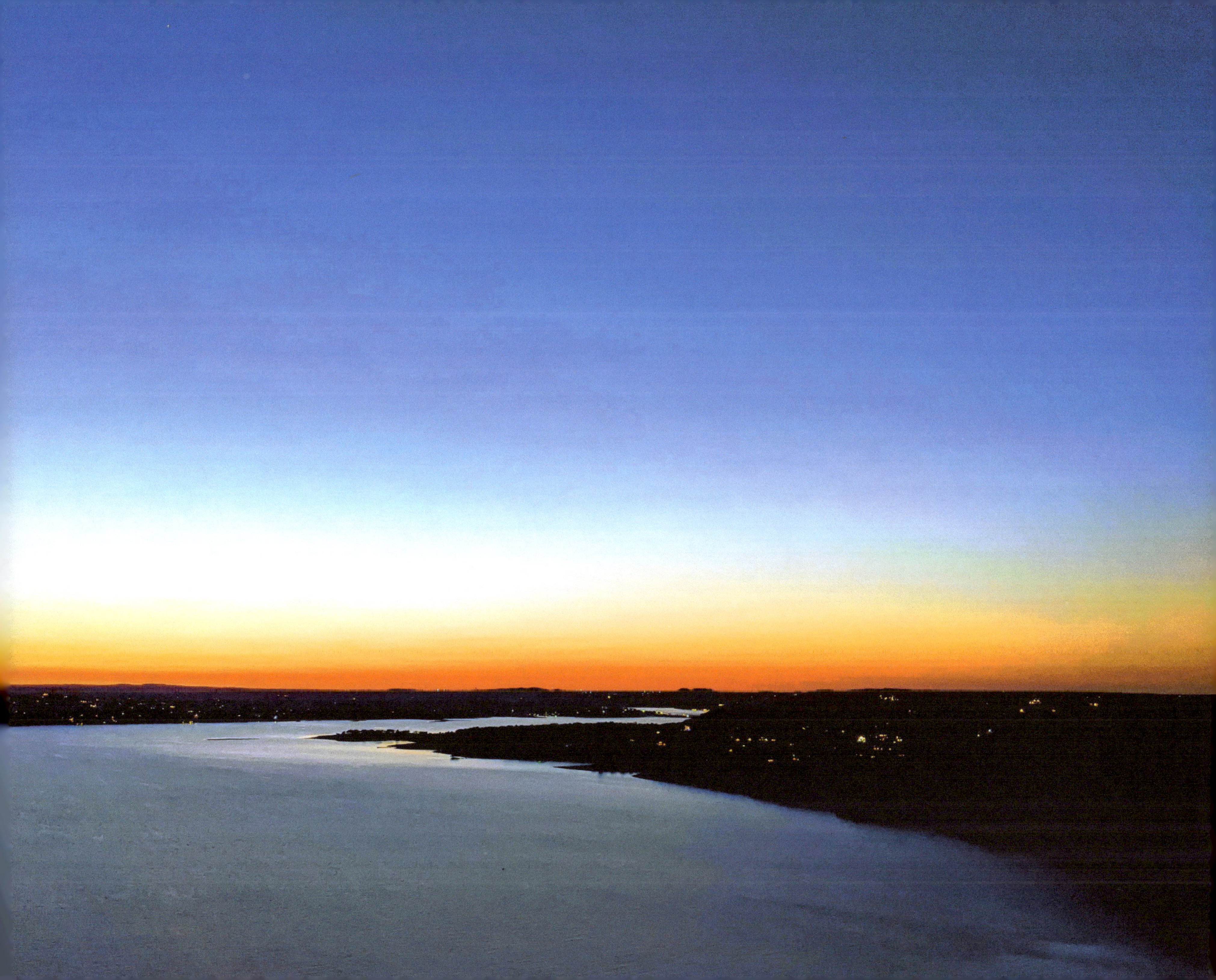

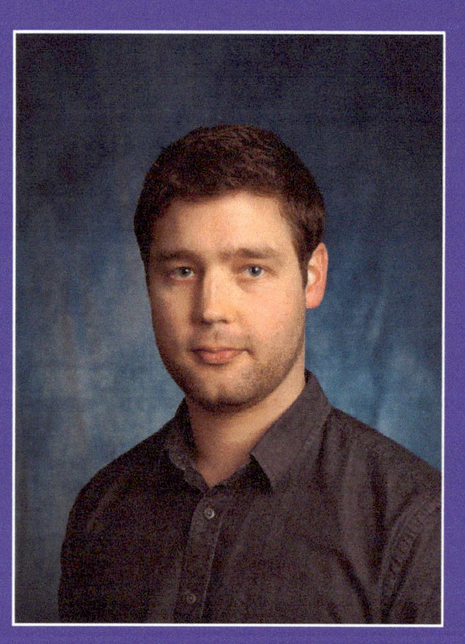

ABOUT THE AUTHOR

Nick Stockland is a Texas Tech graduate, class of 2012. A young professional in the IT consulting industry, currently living in the greatest city in the world – Austin, Texas. Already the author of several children's books, this is Nick's fourth endeavor in photography.